Baa for Beginners

Near

Far

Thin

Fat

Wobbly

Calm

Shivery

Breezy

Bubbly

Ghostly

Breathless

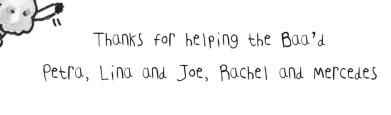

Thanks for helping the Baa'd
Petra, Lina and Joe, Rachel and Mercedes

BAA FOR BEGINNERS
A RED FOX BOOK 978 1 862 30648 6

First published in Great Britain by Hutchinson,
an imprint of Random House Children's Books

Hutchinson edition published 2005
Red Fox edition published 2006

3 5 7 9 10 8 6 4 2

Red Fox Books are published by
Random House Children's Books,
61–63 Uxbridge Road, London W5 5SA,
a division of The Random House Group Ltd,
in Australia by Random House Australia (Pty) Ltd,
20 Alfred Street, Milsons Point, Sydney, NSW 2061, Australia,
in New Zealand by Random House New Zealand Ltd,
18 Poland Road, Glenfield, Auckland 10, New Zealand,
and in South Africa by Random House (Pty) Ltd,
Isle of Houghton, Corner Boundary Road &
Carse O'Gowrie, Houghton 2198, South Africa

THE RANDOM HOUSE GROUP Limited Reg. No. 954009
www.kidsatrandomhouse.co.uk

A CIP catalogue record for this book
is available from the British Library

Printed in Singapore

Baa
for
Beginners

Deborah Fajerman

RED FOX

The language of sheep is called Baa
and every single word is baa.

There are many different ways to speak Baa.

But when sheep are lambs
they only know one kind.

So their teacher Mrs Ramsbottom
takes them on a field trip.

When Baa is near
it's loud and clear.

When Baa is far
it's hard to hear.

When a lamb is all alone,
its baa sounds small and thin . . .

But Baa sounds big
and fat when all the
lambs join in!

Baa is shivery
when it snows . . .

and is whisked right away when the wind blows.

When sheep are climbing
they don't have enough
breath to baaaa . . .

They just huff and puff
and puff and huff.

Baa goes rather wobbly when it's dark as night.

But Baa is calm and flat
when the sun is bright.

When sheep sit on the grass
their bottoms go bright green.

A bubble bath with bubbly baas
makes their bottoms clean.

Mrs Ramsbottom has
finished the field trip.
It is time for the lambs
to take their Baa exam.

They all get a gold star.
And now it's time for their very best baas . . .

The ones they say to their ma's and pa's!

Near

Far

Thin

Fat

Wobbly

Calm

Shivery

Breezy

Bubbly

Ghostly

Breathless

OTHER BOOKS YOU MIGHT ENJOY:

How to Speak Moo!
by Deborah Fajerman

Rodeo Ron and his Milkshake Cows
by Rowan Clifford

Traction Man is Here
by Mini Grey

Where Willy Went
by Nicholas Allan

Yuk!
by Kes Gray and Nick Sharratt

Krong!
by Garry Parsons